Look out for these other exciting titles fro

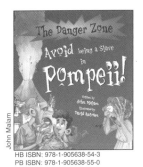

John Malam

HB ISBN: 978-1-905638-54-3
PB ISBN: 978-1-905638-55-0

Fiona Macdonald

HB ISBN: 1-904642-75-6
PB ISBN: 1-904642-76-4

Jacqueline Morley

HB ISBN: 1-905087-55-1
PB ISBN: 1-905087-56-X

Fiona Macdonald

HB ISBN: 978-1-904642-11-4
PB ISBN: 978-1-904642-12-1

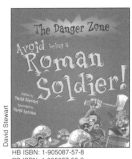

David Stewart

HB ISBN: 1-905087-57-8
PB ISBN: 1-905087-58-6

Fiona Macdonald

HB ISBN: 978-1-905638-79-6
PB ISBN: 978-1-905638-80-2

Simon Smith

HB ISBN: 1-904194-81-8
PB ISBN: 1-904194-82-6

John Malam

HB ISBN: 1-904194-18-4
PB ISBN: 1-904194-19-2

David Stewart

HB ISBN: 1-904194-16-8
PB ISBN: 1-904194-17-6

Peter Cook

HB ISBN: 1-904642-13-6
PB ISBN: 1-904642-14-4

Jacqueline Morley

HB ISBN: 978-1-906370-25-1
PB ISBN: 978-1-906370-26-8

Ian Graham

HB ISBN: 1-904194-55-9
PB ISBN: 1-904194-56-7

Jacqueline Morley

HB ISBN: 1-904642-01-2
PB ISBN: 1-904642-02-0

Michael Ford

HB ISBN: 1-904642-05-5
PB ISBN: 1-904642-06-3

Fiona Macdonald

HB ISBN: 1-904194-53-2
PB ISBN: 1-904194-54-0

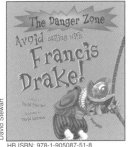

David Stewart

HB ISBN: 978-1-905087-51-8
PB ISBN: 978-1-905087-52-5

Jim Pipe

HB ISBN: 978-1-906714-66-6
PB ISBN: 978-1-906714-67-3

David Stewart

HB ISBN: 978-1-905638-04-8
PB ISBN: 978-1-905638-05-5

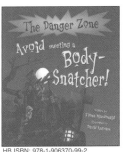

Fiona Macdonald

HB ISBN: 978-1-906370-99-2
PB ISBN: 978-1-906714-00-0

Mark Bergin

HB ISBN: 978-1-905087-61-7
PB ISBN: 978-1-905087-62-4

Fiona Macdonald

HB ISBN: 978-1-904642-07-7
PB ISBN: 978-1-904642-08-4

Fiona Macdonald

HB ISBN: 978-1-905087-49-5
PB ISBN: 978-1-905087-50-1

HB ISBN: 978-1-906714-17-8
PB ISBN: 978-1-906714-18-5

HB ISBN: 978-1-906714-09-3
PB ISBN: 978-1-906714-10-9

John Malam

HB ISBN: 978-1-904642-09-1
PB ISBN: 978-1-904642-10-7

Author:

Richard Humble has written over twenty books on
the history of ships, maritime exploration and naval
history since his first book was published in 1971.
Married with twin daughters, he lives and works in
South Devon, England.

Illustrator:

Mark Bergin was born in Hastings, England, in
1961. He studied at Eastbourne College of Art and
has specialised in historical reconstructions since
leaving art school in 1983.

Series creator:

David Salariya is an illustrator, designer and author.
He is the founder of the Salariya Book Company, which
specialises in the creation and publication of books for
young people, from babies to teenagers, under its
imprints Book House and Scribblers.

Consultant:

Ian Friel is a museum curator and maritime historian.

Editor: **Jenny Millington**

Published by
Book House, an imprint of
The Salariya Book Company Ltd
25 Marlborough Place, Brighton BN1 1UB

SALARIYA

Visit our website at **www.book-house.co.uk**
or go to **www.salariya.com**
for **free** electronic versions of:
You Wouldn't Want to be an Egyptian Mummy!
You Wouldn't Want to be a Roman Gladiator!
You Wouldn't Want to be a Polar Explorer!
You Wouldn't Want to sail on a 19th-Century Whaling Ship!

ISBN 978-1-906714-57-4

A CIP catalogue record for this book is available
from the British Library.

Printed and bound in China.

CONTENTS

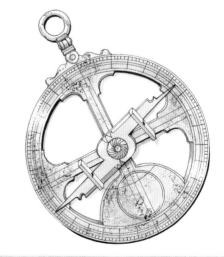

A 16th Century Galleon

Written by
Richard Humble

Series created by
David Salariya

Illustrated by
Mark Bergin

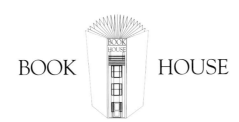

BOOK HOUSE

4

INTRODUCTION

IN THE LATE 16TH CENTURY, European galleons were the latest type of sailing ships. They were taller and far more seaworthy than the oar-driven galleys, and both faster and more powerful than the larger but clumsier carracks of the early 16th century. The galleon was the latest weapon of war at sea, armed with broadside-firing decks of cannon. It was used in battles that changed the history of the world.

Despite the rich cargoes and the splendour of paint and gold leaf, daily life in a galleon was far from romantic. Below decks conditions were cramped and stinking, while on every long voyage rotten food and foul water spread disease. So many men died at sea that new types of rigging had to be invented, so that galleons could be brought home safely by weak and sickly crews. But the romance of the galleon's name lives on.

This book shows how a galleon was built, sailed and navigated, and describes the life and work of galleon designers, craftsmen, builders and crew.

BEFORE THE GALLEON

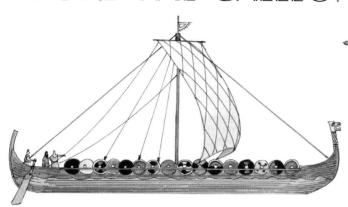

THE GALLEON of the late 16th century was not a completely new type of ship. It developed from two different shipbuilding styles, known as clinker-building and carvel-building (see opposite). During the Middle Ages, from the last years of the Vikings to the time of Columbus, both styles had gone through many changes.

North European ships were built to sail the rough tidal waters of the English Channel, the North and Baltic Seas, and the north-east Atlantic Ocean. They used the same building style as the Vikings: clinker-building, with the hull planks overlapping, and a single mast carrying a square sail. In the 12th century, north European shipbuilders made an important improvement. They replaced the side steering-oar with the stern rudder, a stronger and much more effective method of steering.

Right: French warship of the Crusades, around 1200. Following the same ship-building tradition as the Viking ship, the design was longer and broader to carry large numbers of soldiers, and also horses. The steering-oar of Viking times was still used, but the taller mast was now fixed and braced by side-ropes called *shrouds*. The seal (far right) shows sailors sitting on the yard to help lower the sail.

Viking warriors land from their clinker-built longship. The Viking *hafskip* could either be rowed or sailed. Its sail could be easily raised or lowered.

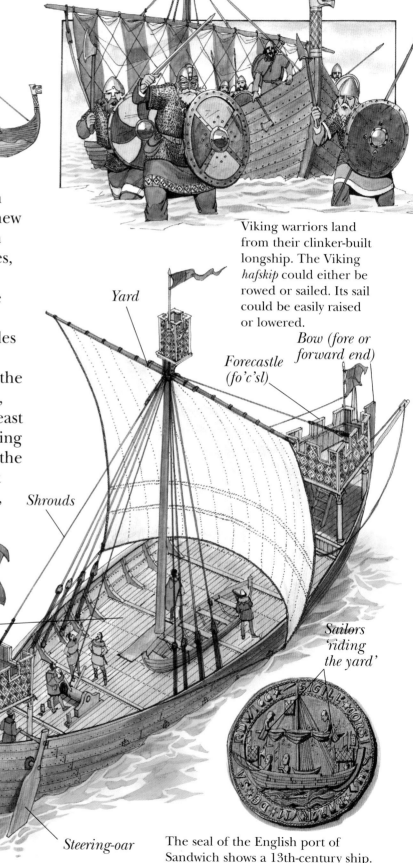

Yard

Forecastle (fo'c'sl)

Bow (fore or forward end)

Shrouds

Amidships

Stern (aft end)

Sailors 'riding the yard'

Sterncastle

Steering-oar

The seal of the English port of Sandwich shows a 13th-century ship.

Above: 14th-century north German cog. This clinker-built ship had an upper deck and a cargo hold.

In the Mediterranean and south-west Europe, medieval ships were built carvel-style, with the planks of the hull laid edge to edge over an inner framework. Instead of a single mast and sail they had two or more masts, carrying triangular *lateen* sails. With these sails a ship could steer into the wind, instead of depending on the wind blowing from the stern (the back of the ship).

Lateen sail   *Square sail*

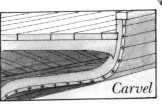

Carvel

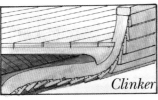

Clinker

Rudder

Carvel building was used in the Mediterranean from about the 8th century onwards. Planks were laid edge to edge, outside a skeleton of frames. The frames could support decks from which guns could fire, through square openings or gunports.

Clinker building, with overlapping planks, was used in northern Europe from the 4th to the 15th centuries.

Above right: By the mid-15th century, the northern and Mediterranean styles were blending. The bow and stern 'castles' of northern ships were being added to carvel-built ships with more than one mast. Caravels (right), used on all the great ocean voyages between about 1460 and 1510, could be rigged with either square sails or triangular lateen sails.

AROUND THE WORLD

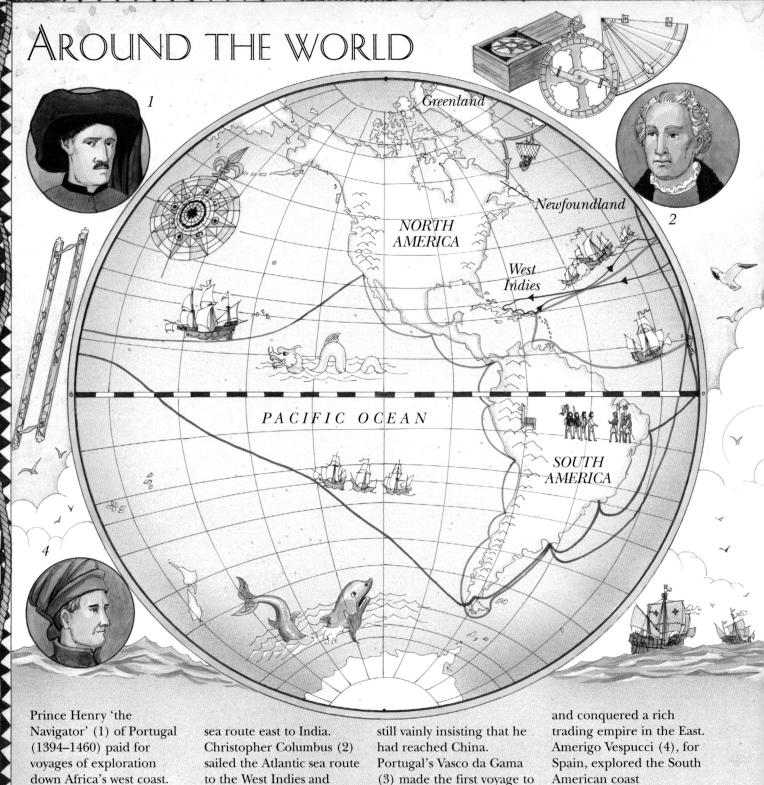

Greenland

Newfoundland

NORTH AMERICA

West Indies

1

2

PACIFIC OCEAN

SOUTH AMERICA

4

Prince Henry 'the Navigator' (1) of Portugal (1394–1460) paid for voyages of exploration down Africa's west coast. These finally opened the sea route east to India. Christopher Columbus (2) sailed the Atlantic sea route to the West Indies and America. He died in 1506, still vainly insisting that he had reached China. Portugal's Vasco da Gama (3) made the first voyage to India and back (1497–1499) and conquered a rich trading empire in the East. Amerigo Vespucci (4), for Spain, explored the South American coast (1499–1501).

THE VIKING explorer Leif Eriksson reached Newfoundland from Greenland around 1001, but his voyage had been long forgotten when ocean exploration began in earnest in the 15th century. By 1480, Portuguese caravels had explored over 3,200 km of Africa's west coast. Under King John II of Portugal (1481–1495) explorers began to search for a sea route around southern Africa to the rich markets of India and China. This route was found by Bartholomew Diaz in 1488–1489. Christopher Columbus sailed from Spain in 1492, seeking a westward short-cut to China across the Atlantic Ocean.

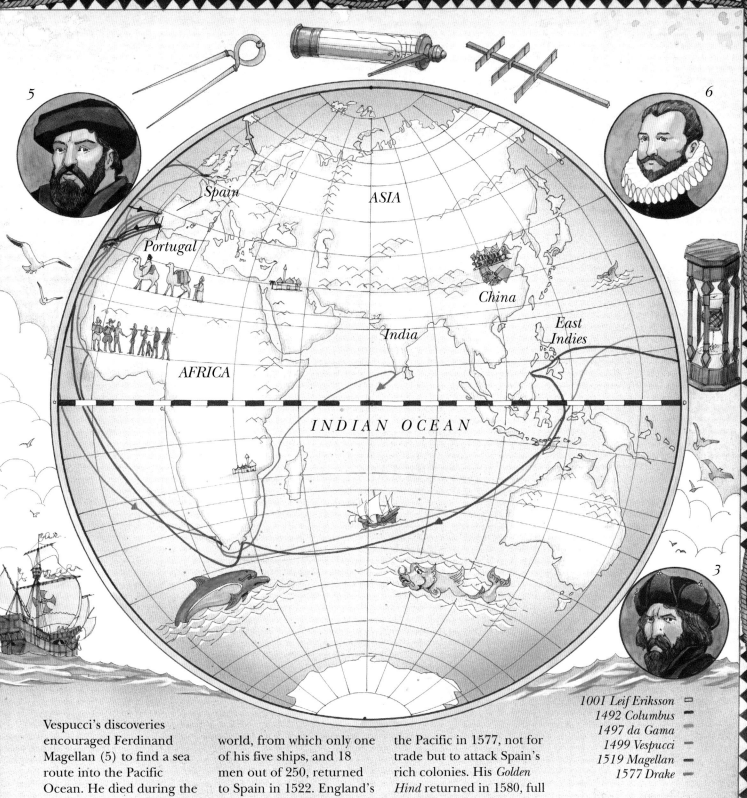

Spain

ASIA

Portugal

China

East
Indies

India

AFRICA

INDIAN OCEAN

1001 *Leif Eriksson*
1492 *Columbus*
1497 *da Gama*
1499 *Vespucci*
1519 *Magellan*
1577 *Drake*

Vespucci's discoveries encouraged Ferdinand Magellan (5) to find a sea route into the Pacific Ocean. He died during the first voyage round the world, from which only one of his five ships, and 18 men out of 250, returned to Spain in 1522. England's Francis Drake (6) sailed for the Pacific in 1577, not for trade but to attack Spain's rich colonies. His *Golden Hind* returned in 1580, full of treasure.

Instead, he discovered the islands of the 'West Indies' and a 'New World' – the American continent. While Spain conquered the West Indies and Central America, Portugal pushed eastwards round Africa and by 1515 had seized the rich spice trade of the East Indies – Europe's first sea-trading empire. In 1519, Spain sent Ferdinand Magellan to make the first crossing of the Pacific Ocean. He died on the journey, but one of his five ships, *Victoria*, completed the first voyage round the world (1519–1522). The feat was not repeated until 1577–1580, by Francis Drake of England in *Golden Hind*.

MARY ROSE, 1545

O N 19 JULY 1545, the English warship *Mary Rose* sank in Portsmouth harbour, in the south of England, as she sailed out to fight the French. From 1979 to 1982, nearly half of the hull and hundreds of personal items were recovered from the seabed. It was a wonderful discovery. Nothing else has revealed so much about 16th-century ships.

Mary Rose was built for King Henry VIII of England. He wanted a modern war fleet, with warships able to use the new cannon, but still carrying soldiers and archers as warships had done throughout the Middle Ages. Heavy guns would beat down resistance before the enemy ship was boarded and captured.

Mary Rose was intended for short war cruises in the English Channel, not for long ocean voyages. She was built in 1510–1511, then rebuilt in 1536 to carry more and heavier guns. Her design was like that of a late 15th-century trading carrack, strengthened to add decks of guns. These fired through square ports cut in the ship's sides. On that last day, *Mary Rose* set sail with her gunports open and her cannon loaded ready to fire. Then she rolled over too far to one side, perhaps because of bad seamanship, and water rushed in through the open gunports of the lower deck. The ship sank quickly, and most of the crew were lost.

Sir George Carew (1), Vice-Admiral of the Fleet, who went down with *Mary Rose*. His last words, shouted to a relative passing in a nearby ship, show that bad discipline was partly to blame for the disaster: 'I have the sort of knaves I cannot rule!' Even in the cannon age, England relied heavily on the rapid fire of archers (2) armed with the deadly longbow.

The *Mary Rose* wreck contained 2,500 arrows and 139 complete longbows. Archers carried their arrows (3) in bundles of 24, held in round leather 'spacers' to prevent damage to the feathers. A bone tip (4) was fitted to the end of the bow, grooved for the string. A leather bracer (5) protected the archer's forearm from the slap of the released bowstring.

The castle decks (6), and the broad ship's 'waist' or middle section, were covered with light timbers that supported netting to stop enemies climbing aboard.

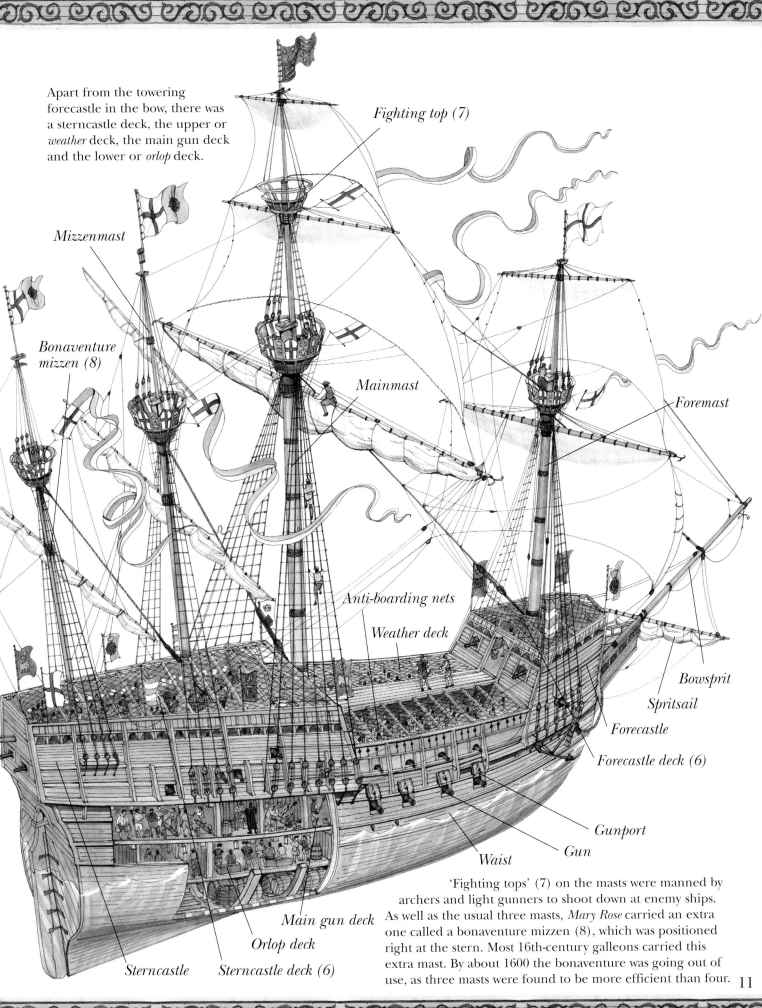

Apart from the towering forecastle in the bow, there was a sterncastle deck, the upper or *weather* deck, the main gun deck and the lower or *orlop* deck.

Fighting top (7)

Mizzenmast

Bonaventure mizzen (8)

Mainmast

Foremast

Anti-boarding nets

Weather deck

Bowsprit

Spritsail

Forecastle

Forecastle deck (6)

Gunport

Gun

Waist

Main gun deck

Orlop deck

Sterncastle

Sterncastle deck (6)

'Fighting tops' (7) on the masts were manned by archers and light gunners to shoot down at enemy ships. As well as the usual three masts, *Mary Rose* carried an extra one called a bonaventure mizzen (8), which was positioned right at the stern. Most 16th-century galleons carried this extra mast. By about 1600 the bonaventure was going out of use, as three masts were found to be more efficient than four.

LIFE ON BOARD

IN FOUR YEARS of careful excavation on the seabed (1979–1982), divers recovered more than 17,000 objects from *Mary Rose*. They are marvellous evidence of how a 16th-century warship was built and armed, and of the lifestyle of her soldiers and crew.

Instead of the 415 sailors, gunners and soldiers she was supposed to carry, about 700 men were packed aboard *Mary Rose* on that last day. She sank so quickly that many were trapped below decks, and only about 30 were saved. When found over 400 years later, the wreck still held the bones of drowned crewmen, the bones, pips and shells of the meat, fish, fruit and nuts they ate, the dice and domino games they played – even the pipes with which they made music.

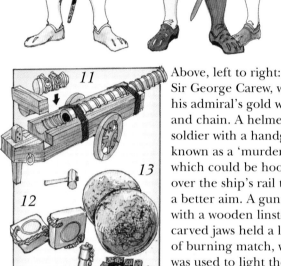

Below: Some tableware.
(1) Drinking flagon.
(2) Plate, knife and spoon.
(3) Candlestick. (4) Wooden beer mug. (5) Pepper mill.
(6) Holder for peppercorns.

Below right: Officers' personal kit. (7) Folding manicure set.
(8) Comb and thimble.
(9) Spice-stuffed pomander (sniffed to mask nasty smells).
(10) Carved bone scoops for cleaning out the ears.

Right: Some weapons.
(11) Iron maindeck gun on wooden carriage, with gunpowder firing-chamber.
(12) Mould for casting lead shot. (13) Stone roundshot.
(14) Bronze-topped gunpowder horn. (15) Small squareshot for the 'murderer' handgun shown above. (16) Heavy bronze muzzle-loading gun.
(17) Carved linstock.

Above, left to right: Sir George Carew, wearing his admiral's gold whistle and chain. A helmeted soldier with a handgun known as a 'murderer', which could be hooked over the ship's rail to give a better aim. A gunner with a wooden linstock. Its carved jaws held a length of burning match, which was used to light the gunpowder when firing the guns.

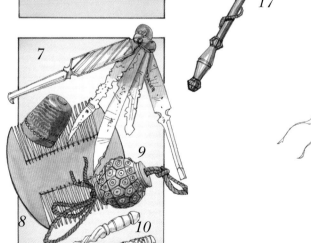

The barber-surgeon (left), with a selection of the 64 items found packed in his medicine chest.

This is the oldest known example of how medical care was provided at sea in the age of the galleon.

Among the more important officers of *Mary Rose* was a medical doctor, known as a barber-surgeon. In the wreckage of his cabin on the maindeck, divers found his medicine chest intact – with all its contents apart from the steel blades, which had rusted away. The barber-surgeon's chest contained 64 items. These included jars with ointment still inside, drug flasks, syringes, a bowl and a small mallet (possibly used for knocking out the patient before an operation). One of the barber-surgeon's distinctive velvet caps was found and successfully restored.

Even the remains of the ship's pests – rats, fleas and weevils – were found aboard *Mary Rose*.

It is thought that the frog lived in the water barrel, to show that the water was fresh!

A NEW GALLEON TAKES SHAPE

THE GALLEON that led the English fleet against the Spanish Armada in 1588, *Ark Royal*, was built just 40 years after *Mary Rose* sank. Many lessons had been learned since that disaster and galleons were now lighter and not so tall. Sir Walter Raleigh (1554–1618), the rich English courtier who had *Ark Royal* built, wrote that building ships too high above the water 'makes them labour and makes them overset' (makes them top-heavy, hard to handle and even likely to capsize).

Here we show a galleon nearing completion just after the time of the Armada, around 1590. Compared with the ill-fated *Mary Rose*, the most obvious difference is that there are no towering bow and stern castles. With less high structure above decks, the new galleon design gave less resistance to the wind. This enabled the galleon to sail faster, and to steer more directly into the wind than earlier large ships.

A 16th-century shipyard was a hive of activity, swarming with workmen skilled in many trades. No other industry of the day employed so many workmen in so small a space. A new ship could either be built for launching from a slipway, as here, or in a dry-dock which was flooded when the ship was ready to be floated out.

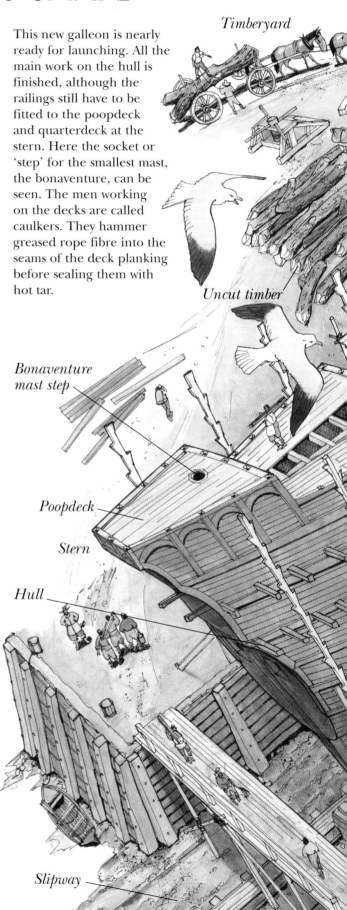

Timberyard

Uncut timber

Bonaventure mast step

Poopdeck

Stern

Hull

Slipway

This new galleon is nearly ready for launching. All the main work on the hull is finished, although the railings still have to be fitted to the poopdeck and quarterdeck at the stern. Here the socket or 'step' for the smallest mast, the bonaventure, can be seen. The men working on the decks are called caulkers. They hammer greased rope fibre into the seams of the deck planking before sealing them with hot tar.

A new galleon was launched without masts, rigging or guns. These were added later, when the ship was 'fitted out'. A galleon might be built and launched in one place, receive the masts and rigging there, then sail to another location to take aboard new guns.

In a 16th-century shipyard, the place where a new ship was built had several specialist workshops nearby. There was a timberyard, where trunks of oak and elm were stored. From here, timbers were taken to the saw-pit to be cut to size as required by the shipwright's plans. Smithies supplied the nails and bolts needed to fix the timbers together. Tar-boilers prepared the hot pitch that waterproofed the joints between every plank in the hull and deck. Cables and ropes for the rigging were made in the rope-walks.

Caulkers   Quarterdeck

Weather deck

Foredeck   Scaffolding

Bow

Ladder

Rope

15

THE TIMBERYARD

IN THEORY, a modern shipwright could use a computer to design a ship to be built in any size, shape or materials. But 400 years ago, working only with wood, designing a ship was a very skilled craft.

No two galleons were ever exactly the same, even when built to the same basic design. The reason was simple: no two trees grow in exactly the same shape. When drawing up plans for a new galleon, the only thing a shipwright knew for certain was that he would be working with two sorts of wooden pieces.

The first was 'straight timber', needed in different lengths for parts like the keel, the sternpost, and the rudder. The second was called 'compass' or 'crooked timber': lengths of wood cut to use the strongest natural curve of the wood. This was used for curved parts of the ship's frames, and for the naturally curved wooden brackets, or *knees*, that joined a galleon's decks to the sides of the ship.

A galleon's 'skeleton' was a row of U-shaped frames fastened to the keel. These were made smaller at each end of the keel to form the ship's bow and stern. As every joint is a point of weakness, the shipwright always tried to design a ship with frames made of the fewest possible pieces (known as *futtocks*) of crooked timber.

Above: The master shipwright views the plans of a new ship.

Knee

Shapes of finished timbers

Left: An expert could 'see' finished timbers of many shapes before the mature tree had even been felled.

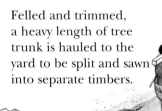

Felled and trimmed, a heavy length of tree trunk is hauled to the yard to be split and sawn into separate timbers.

Four-man team carrying a barrel of pitch. Its solid contents will be chopped out in pieces and melted in a cauldron over a fire.

Above: The busy scene at a ship-building timberyard shows the frames of a new galleon rising on the slipway beyond.

Right: Rough timber being cut into square sections in the saw-pits. A long saw was used by two men, one standing on the timber and one in a hole (or pit) in the ground beneath. Together they pulled and pushed the saw up and down.

Below: On the floor of a shed called the *mould-loft*, completed futtocks are laid out on the floor, then joined to form the U-shaped curve of a large ship's frame.

Right: Patterns cut from light planking were called *moulds*. Here one is used to trace the exact outline of a new futtock onto the timber from which it will be cut in the saw-pit.

A day in the life of a shipyard worker

Beer for breakfast as a shipyard carpenter prepares for another day's work.

Shouldering his adze, the carpenter walks to the yard. He meets a workmate on the way.

They look at the pond in which timber for new masts is softened by soaking before being trimmed to shape.

The master shipwright tells the men which timbers are to be worked on and completed today.

Laying the mould for a frame section on a piece of rough timber that seems to have the right length and curve.

An iron-hard oak knot has bitten a notch out of the adze blade. The blacksmith will soon put that right.

Midday, after five hours of hard work. Time for the men's dinner break: bread and cheese, eaten in the workshop.

Back to work. The new timber is shaping up nicely, its surface smoothed by skilful strokes of the razor-sharp adze.

The master shipwright greets some important visitors – the merchants who will be paying for the new ship to be built.

At the end of the day, the new piece of timber is finished and is ready for checking by the master shipwright.

A well-earned rest. The timberyard workers wash away the taste of wood-dust with a few tankards of ale at the inn!

Home again, after a working day which, in midsummer, will probably have lasted twelve hours or more.

18

RISING FROM THE KEEL

EVEN TODAY, a new ship's life is said to begin when it is 'laid down'. This means laying down the keel, which for a galleon was usually of elm wood. Even a medium-sized galleon needed a keel 30 metres long, so the keel was nearly always made of several lengths joined together.

The straight sternpost and the curving stem were then fixed to either end of the keel. In between, running across the keel, the floor timbers were laid. These shaped the flat underside of the ship at its widest point. Then the curved fashion-pieces provided the outline of the ship's stern. They were linked by the sturdy transom, which ran from side to side across the sternpost.

Next came the raising of the curved frames, or ribs, shaping the outline of the ship's sides. To these were added the stout knees (angled pieces) supporting the deck-beams running across the ship. Outside, the work of planking began, forming the ship's 'skin'. Laying the planks carvel-style, edge to edge, made it possible for the square ports to be cut, through which the galleon's guns would fire. A new galleon could be ready for launching in six months from the time the keel was laid down.

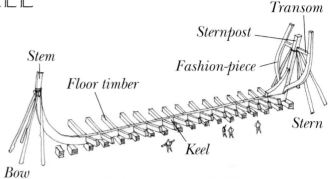

First stages: laying the keel and adding the stem, sternpost, floor timbers, fashion-pieces and transom.

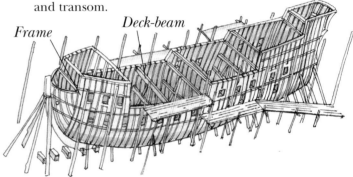

With every frame raised from the keel, the knees are added and the ship's sides are joined by the deck beams.

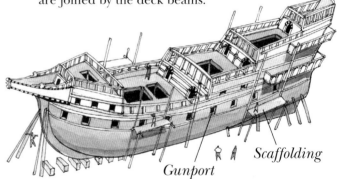

Once the side planking is complete, the square ports for the galleon's guns are cut in the sides at deck level.

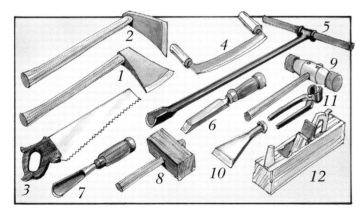

Carpenter's tools: (1) axe; (2) adze for smoothing surfaces; (3) saw; (4) drawknife for rounding off timber; (5) auger for boring holes; (6) chisel; (7) gouge; (8) mallet; (9) caulking hammer; (10) caulking iron; (11) pincers; (12) plane.

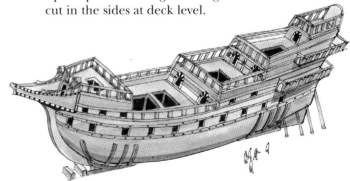

The new galleon is ready to be launched. All the seams are caulked and watertight, and the scaffolding has been taken down.

An army of craftsmen

The shipwrights (below) drew the plans and supervised the building of the ship.

Sawyers spent weary hours in the saw-pits, cutting timbers and planking from lengths of iron-hard oak.

Carpenter and joiner. The joiner's craft was cutting tongues and sockets to join timbers.

Blacksmiths' forges provided the ironwork: from bolts and brackets to heavy rudder-pintles.

A BUSY SHIPYARD gave regular employment to scores of people: craftsmen, boy apprentices learning their trade, and suppliers of raw materials. The suppliers were hardly less important than the craftsmen working on the ships. They provided everything from timber to hemp for ropes and cables, iron for the nailmakers, smiths and coopers, and pitch for the caulkers. Many of these materials had to be brought from overseas and supplying them to the yards was an important trade in itself.

Shipyard workers did not have to rely only on building new ships. There was constant work repairing and rebuilding existing ships.

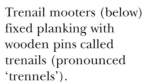

Trenail mooters (below) fixed planking with wooden pins called trenails (pronounced 'trennels').

Another coil of new rope for the rigging is brought to the ship by a pair of rope-walk boys.

Mastmakers at work (above), planing off the angles to make a new mast.

'Scavelman' (above right) was the name given to the humblest type of dockyard labourer.

One of the teamsters (below), whose horses and carts moved the heaviest loads to wherever they were needed.

A pitch-heater tends the fire beneath the cauldron preparing more tar for waterproofing plank seams.

Wheels for the gun-carriages, whether solid or spoked, were made by the wheelwright.

Coopers made the hundreds of casks and barrels to hold gun-powder, food or drink.

The English galleon *Ark Royal*, built in 1586–1587, fought the Spanish Armada in 1588. Twenty years later she was rebuilt and renamed *Anne Royal* after the new Queen. She sailed on her last expedition in 1625, and was only sunk by accident in 1636.

Some of the ships of the Spanish Armada were probably built in the Basque region of northern Spain. The Basque shipbuilders were well known for the high standard of their work and could take advantage of the plentiful local supplies of oak timber and iron. Their ships not only sailed to war, but were used on expeditions to hunt for whales, as well as on the trading routes between Spain and France.

The sailmaker (below left) cut and stitched the sails, adding lengths of rope to give them extra strength.

Riggers prepared the ship's complicated web of ropes and rigging. They were expert at splicing ropes.

The blockmaker made the pulleys and heavy blocks essential for working the ship's rigging, to raise and lower the sails.

A caulker at work, hammering in lengths of greased rope fibres to seal a planking seam.

GUNS, SAILS AND ROPES

THE DEMAND for powerful, accurate guns for warships led to great changes in 16th-century metalworking. When England's *Mary Rose* was lost in 1545, her best guns were cast in expensive bronze (a mixture of copper and tin). But by 1600 most guns were cast in a cheaper way, using iron.

The heaviest gun mounted in galleons was the demi-cannon, about 3 metres long and firing a shot weighing about 14.5 kg. The type of gun most suited for galleons was the demi-culverin. This was sometimes as long as 3.5 metres, although by the 1590s shorter versions were coming into use.

Guns were cast by pouring molten metal into a mould. Bronze was easier to cast but the high cost of copper made it expensive. Iron was more plentiful and so was far cheaper to cast.

Here (right) a new gun is being polished. The men in the background are swinging up the wood-cased mould for a new gun barrel.

Yarns being twisted into strands

Strands being twisted into rope

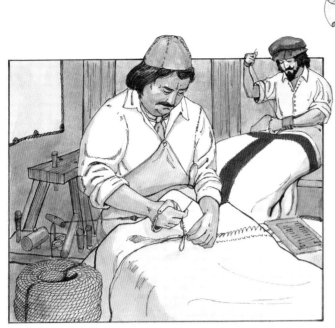

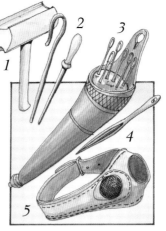

Left: Ropemakers' tools. The serving mallet (1) was used to wrap an outer layer of yarn tightly round a rope, to make it more waterproof. The prickers (2) were used to adjust rope strands to lie correctly in place.

The sailmaker's craft had its own language. A square sail had a *head* (upper edge) and a curved *foot*; each side was called the *leech*, and the centre or curved belly was the *bunt*. The sail's upper corners were fixed to the yard by *earings*; the bottom corners were the *clews*. Triangular sails were usually made in two pieces. These were joined and strengthened by a seam called the *mitre*.

'Rope' was the name for all cords more than 2.5 cm thick. The ropemakers spun hemp fibres right-handed into yarns, twisted them left-handed into strands, then twisted three or more strands right-handed into rope.

The sailmaker (above) was a vital member of every crew. His job was to keep every sail in good repair, not only mending torn sails but making new ones when required.

Top right: Sailmakers' tools. The bullock's horn (3), packed with tallow, or fat, to hold the big needles (4), could be hung from a belt. The sailmaker's 'palm' (5) was a flat, thick thimble, worn on the palm to push the needles through the cloth.

Rope-makers at work. The strands being twisted left-handed are then twisted or 'laid up' the other way to make the finished rope.

LAUNCHING A NEW GALLEON

THE LAUNCH of a new galleon was always a very special occasion, a moment for pride and celebration. The sight of the new ship, afloat at last, was the first real proof that all the time and money put into her planning and building had not been wasted.

A galleon built in a dry dock might have her lower masts fitted before the launch, or this might be done as the launched ship lay at the dockside. Once afloat, the ship was carefully balanced in the water by laying heavy ballast stones in the bottom of the ship, on either side of the keel. Then the work of fitting the new ship's masts and rigging began, in preparation for the first trial voyage.

Many famous galleons were ordered, built, and paid for by wealthy subjects in order to earn favour with the monarch. A good example was the *Galleon Leicester*, built in 1582 on the orders of the Earl of Leicester, one of the favourite courtiers of Elizabeth I. *Galleon Leicester* sailed with the English fleet against the Spanish Armada in 1588. The Spanish fleet included the *Florencia*, which had been built by the Duke of Tuscany, in Italy. The Duke named his ship *San Francesco*, and used her to trade in spices, but she was seized by the Spanish navy, given a new name and sent to war.

The year is 1586, and a syndicate or partnership of rich courtiers has put up the money to build a new galleon. It will sail on trading voyages, or carry out attacks on enemy shipping. All the members of the syndicate will take a share of the profits.

Here they assemble on the dockside with their ladies to admire their new ship.

When hiring sailors for any voyage, the captain would be anxious to find men with as much sea experience as possible. Sailors who were expert at working and repairing the upper rigging, in all weathers, were always eagerly sought. Sailors were never keen to sail on an especially dangerous journey. Sometimes the captain lied to the men about where they would be going on a voyage. By the time the men discovered the truth, it would be too late to do anything about it.

These sailors are about to join the crew of a new Spanish galleon. Their names are listed by a ship's officer. They describe their experience and the skills they have learned on previous sea voyages.

Preparing for Sea

WHILE THE MASTS were 'stepped' (fitted into their sockets) and the rigging set up, the caulkers finished the waterproofing of the last planking seams. Meanwhile, the stores needed for the voyage – powder and shot for the guns, spare timbers, ropes and sailcloth, casks of salt meat, fish, water, beer and wine – would be arriving on the dockside ready for checking and storing below decks.

Cranes called 'sheerlegs' were set up on deck for the difficult job of coaxing the lower masts down through the decks, to rest in the sockets made for them above the keel. They were then wedged in place and braced up on deck by stout guy-ropes known as shrouds.

When complete, each mast consisted of three linked sections: lower mast, topmast and topgallant mast. Teams of sailors hauling on lifting tackles hoisted the upper masts into position. Once the masts were fully set up and secured, the yards were hoisted in turn and supported by slings. The sails were then fastened to the yards.

If a galleon was not needed for a long period, she would be left at anchor with her topgallant and topmasts lowered and stored away to prevent unnecessary wear and tear from the weather. The ship was then said to be 'laid up'.

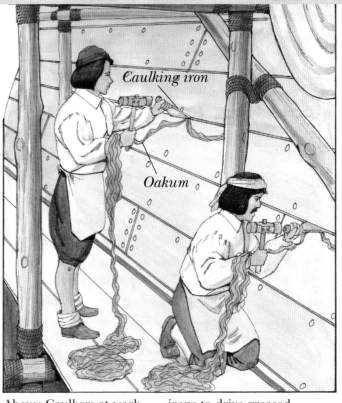

Above: Caulkers at work, using hammers and sharp-edged caulking irons to drive greased oakum (hemp fibre) between the planks.

Right: A galleon's mizzenmast is carefully lowered until, far below, its foot enters the step or socket above the keel. It was always a difficult job, with the risk of the lifting tackle breaking and the mast plunging like a spear through the bottom of the ship. Once stepped, the mast was wedged solidly into holes cut for it in each deck.

Heavy supporting ropes called shrouds, fanning out from the masthead, were then secured to chains fixed to the ship's sides. When the lower masts were fixed in place, the topmasts and topgallant masts were hoisted up. Ratlines, running across the shrouds like the rungs of a ladder, helped the men climb to the masthead safely.

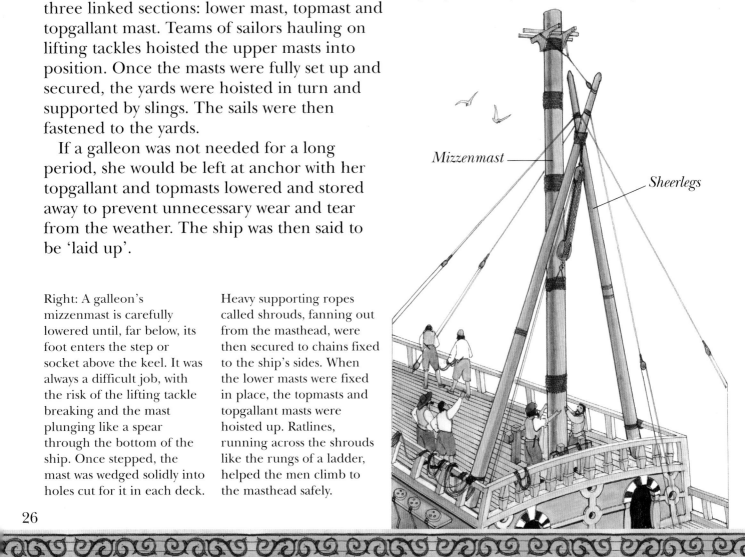

Topgallant masts

Topmasts

Shrouds

Main yard-arm

Ratlines

Caulking and rigging are complete, and the galleon is ready to be loaded with stores. The main yard-arm acts as a crane for hoisting the heavier loads.

INSIDE THE BOW

THE BOW or forward section of a galleon was where the ship's crew or 'people' lived on board. 'Forecastle' or 'fo'c'sl hands' remained a familiar term for a ship's crew throughout the age of sail.

In this galleon, soldiers can be seen at drill on the upper forecastle deck, while a gunner checks one of the light swivel guns mounted on the ship's rail. One deck down, on the upper or weather deck, the ship's gunners are also being put through their paces. On the maindeck below, to the right, a gunner's mate is checking the tackle of one of the maindeck guns.

Standing out from the weather deck is one of the ship's capstans or winches, used to shift heavy weights on deck or up in the rigging. They were turned by teams of men, pushing stout wooden staves fitted into the head of the capstan. One deck down, the ship's main capstan can be seen mounted on the maindeck. Its most important function was to haul up the ship's anchors at the moment of sailing. On the lowest deck, the orlop, seamen are checking to see that the anchor cable has been correctly coiled down in the cable tier.

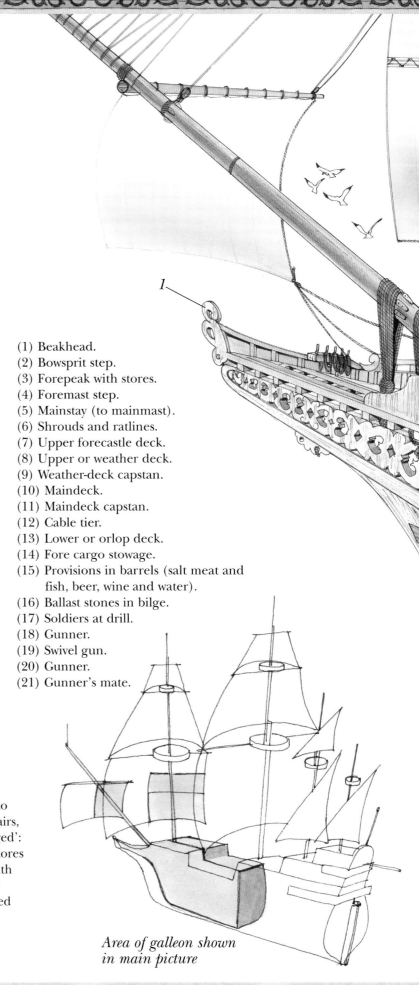

(1) Beakhead.
(2) Bowsprit step.
(3) Forepeak with stores.
(4) Foremast step.
(5) Mainstay (to mainmast).
(6) Shrouds and ratlines.
(7) Upper forecastle deck.
(8) Upper or weather deck.
(9) Weather-deck capstan.
(10) Maindeck.
(11) Maindeck capstan.
(12) Cable tier.
(13) Lower or orlop deck.
(14) Fore cargo stowage.
(15) Provisions in barrels (salt meat and fish, beer, wine and water).
(16) Ballast stones in bilge.
(17) Soldiers at drill.
(18) Gunner.
(19) Swivel gun.
(20) Gunner.
(21) Gunner's mate.

Area of galleon shown in main picture

Life on board a galleon could be very unpleasant. Below decks the smell was terrible – not just from dirty bodies and clothes, but from all the ship's filth, which ended up in the bilge with the ballast stones. On long voyages, when it was necessary to beach the ship for repairs, she would be 'rummaged': emptied of guns and stores and scrubbed clean, with the filthy ballast stones thrown out and replaced with clean ones.

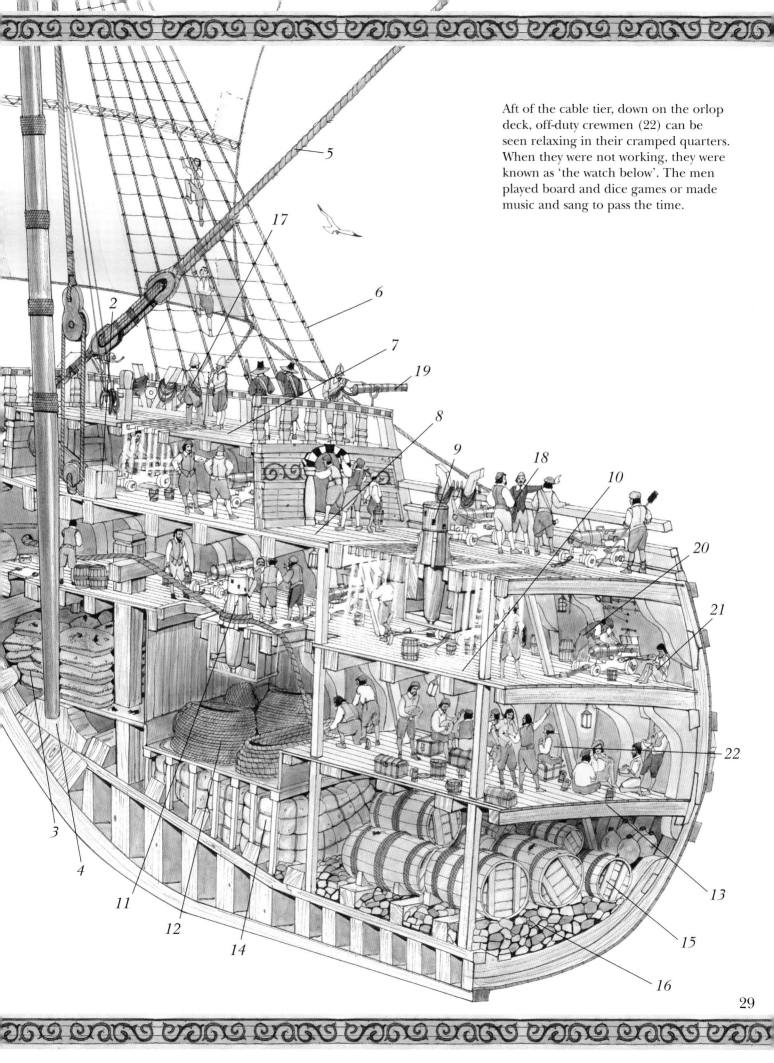

5

17

2

6

7

19

8

9

18

10

20

21

3

4

11

12

14

13

15

16

22

Aft of the cable tier, down on the orlop deck, off-duty crewmen (22) can be seen relaxing in their cramped quarters. When they were not working, they were known as 'the watch below'. The men played board and dice games or made music and sang to pass the time.

INSIDE THE STERN

THE MOST COMFORTABLE area of a galleon lay aft of the waist (the ship's centre section). It was here in the stern that the galleon's officers and passengers had their cramped cabins and the ship was steered.

A galleon had no steering-wheel; this did not come into widespread use until the early 18th century. Instead the galleon was steered with a *whipstaff*. This was a long lever running down through the deck and connected by a hinge called the goose-neck to the tiller – the lever which moved the rudder from side to side. The whipstaff was operated by the helmsman, who was below decks and so could not see outside the ship. Here the helmsman can be seen at (14), just astern of the mizzenmast. The captain has ordered a change of course, which is being shouted down to the helmsman through a small hatchway.

All the ship's provisions were stored near the galley, where the food was prepared. Fire aboard ship was a constant danger, and the galley fire, despite the protection of its brick furnace, was only lit for short periods when the sea was not too rough. Most food was cooked by boiling. But when the sea was rough, there was no hot food.

(1) Starboard main shrouds.
(2) Mizzen stay. (3) Mizzenmast.
(4) Starboard mizzen shrouds.
(5) Bonaventure stay.
(6) Bonaventure mast.
(7) Starboard bonaventure shrouds. (8) Poopdeck.
(9) Upper stern gallery.
(10) Quarterdeck. (11) 'Great Cabin', for captain or admiral.
(12) Bonaventure step.
(13) Lower stern gallery.
(14) Helmsman and whipstaff.
(15) Gooseneck. (16) Tiller.

(17) Rudder, hung on hooked pintles. (18) Heavy gun firing through stern (stern-chaser).
(19) Upper or weather deck.
(20) Maindeck. (21) Aft capstan.
(22) Hatch to orlop deck.
(23) Cabin. (24) Lower or orlop deck. (25) Sailmaker's store.
(26) Cook and boy helpers in galley. (27) Brick furnace for galley fire, with cauldron boiling salt meat. (28) Provisions in barrels. (29) Mizzenmast step.
(30) Ballast in bilge. (31) Keel.

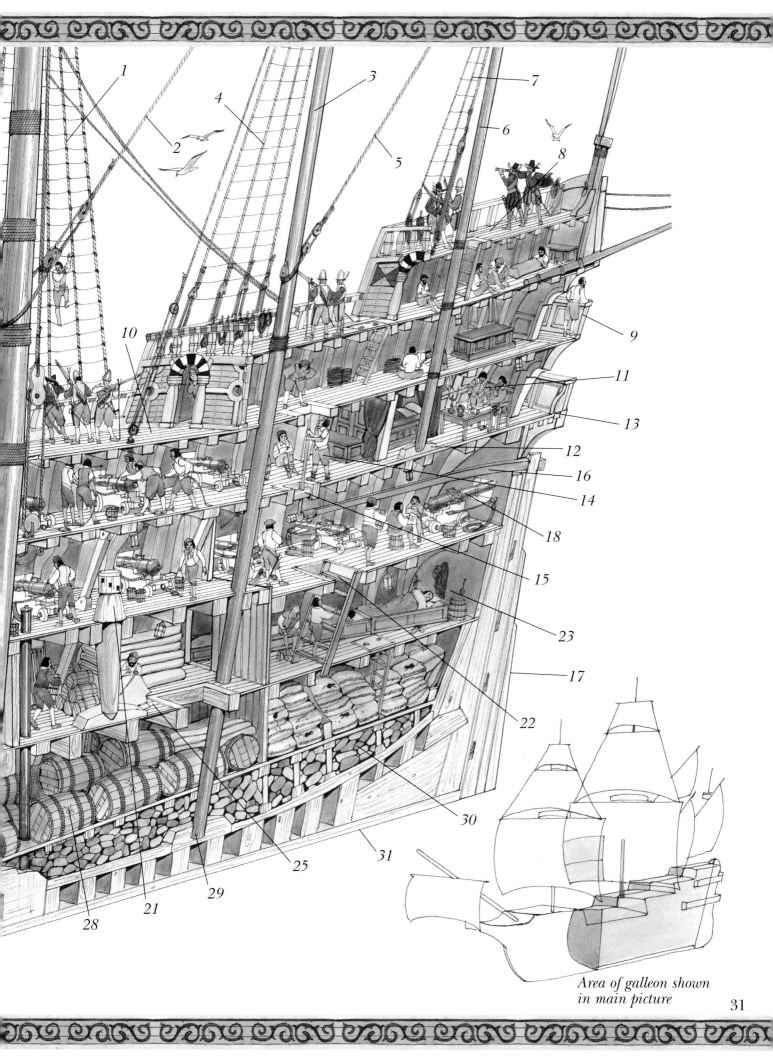

Area of galleon shown
in main picture

HOW THE RIGGING WORKED

THERE WERE TWO types of tackle in a galleon's rigging, and these were known as the standing rigging and the running rigging. The standing rigging included the shrouds on either side of the masts, and the stays running between the masts. The standing rigging held up the masts and braced them firmly in position.

The running rigging took its name from the blocks and pulleys through which the ropes ran, and which made their work more efficient. The running rigging included the halyards, used for hoisting and lowering sails.

Sheets and tacks kept the sails taut. Braces swung the yards to get the most advantage when the wind shifted direction.

The long ocean voyages made during the 16th century led to great changes in the rigging of ships. On such voyages there were always many deaths from sickness, accidents or battle. A homeward-bound galleon would nearly always have far fewer crewmen than at the start of the voyage. More and more block-and-pulley tackles were therefore used as labour-saving devices. These made it possible for the surviving sailors to sail the ship home.

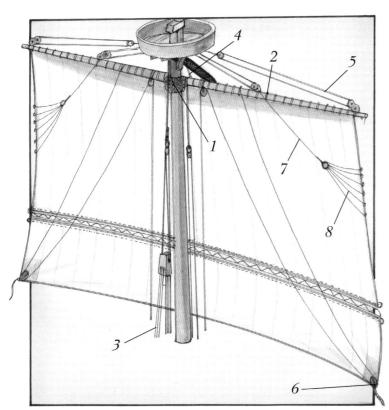

The rigging of a galleon's main yard. The parrel (1) held the yard against the mast. Robbands (2) fastened the sail to the yard. Halyards (3) hoisted the yard up the mast, to where the ties (4) and lifts (5) held it in place. Sheets (6), fixed to the sail's lower corners, kept it full with each shift of the wind. In strong winds, when the sail had to be shortened to save it from damage, the martnets (7) and clewlines (8) bunched the sail up against the yard.

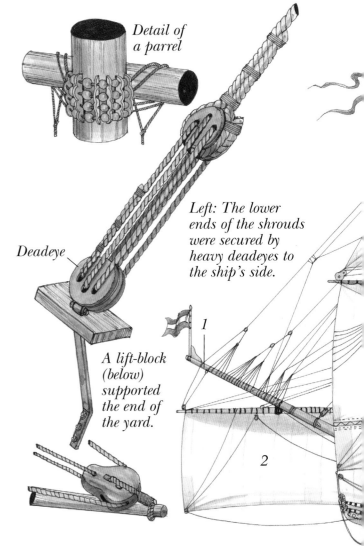

Detail of a parrel

Deadeye

Left: The lower ends of the shrouds were secured by heavy deadeyes to the ship's side.

A lift-block (below) supported the end of the yard.

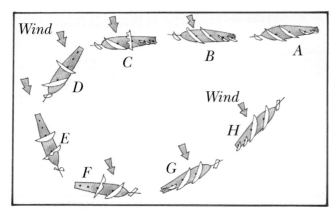

Left: How swinging the yards round helped a ship change course. The yards are braced (A, B, C) to make full use of the wind blowing from the starboard. As the ship turns its stern to the wind (D, E) the yards are braced square. As the ship settles on its new course (F, G, H) with the wind now blowing from the port side, the yards are braced the opposite way to (A–C).

Below: On this Dutch galleon of about 1610, the foresail, mainsail and mizzensail have been deepened with *bonnets*: laced-on sections added to give sails extra pulling power in steady winds.

(1) Bowsprit. (2) Spritsail. (3) Main topgallant stay. (4) Main and mizzen topmast stays. (5) Main, mizzen and bonaventure stays. (6) Fore and main topgallant sails. (7) Fore, main and mizzen topsails. (8) Fore and main courses (square). (9) Mizzen and bonaventure sails (lateen). (10) Fore, main and mizzen topmast shrouds. (11) Fore, main, mizzen and bonaventure shrouds. (12) Bonnets.

OFFICERS AND CREW

NO TWO GALLEONS were identical, and no two galleons put to sea with the same numbers of officers and crewmen. A galleon sailing as part of a war fleet would have far more soldiers and trained gunners on board than a ship on a trading cruise.

Although the captain was responsible for the success of the voyage, he was often a gentleman with no training in seamanship or navigation. He would rely heavily on the master, always a trained seaman and navigator, who directed the efficient working of the ship. Large galleons would probably have a trained surgeon on board; smaller ones would not. An admiral might have his own musicians, such as trumpeters, as well as the ship's drummer-boy and fife (small flute) players.

But every galleon had its expert craftsmen: men like the ship's carpenter, sailmaker, cook and cooper. The cooper was one of the most important men aboard, for he was in charge of the barrels and casks storing all the food and drink. If a lazy or drunken cooper let the casks leak, the food would rot, wine and beer would go sour, and the water would become undrinkable early in the voyage. This would probably mean that more crewmen would die before the voyage was over.

Left and below: Some of the officers and crew of a typical galleon.
(1) Captain. (2) Ship's master (and second navigating officer).
(3) Musketeer.
(4) Ship's carpenter.

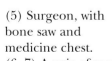

5

11

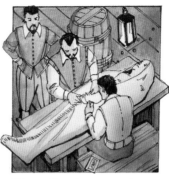

A broken rope sends a sailor falling to his death from the upper rigging onto the deck below.

The sailmaker sews the dead man into his hammock, weighted with shot to make it sink.

The captain reads the burial service as the body is slid over the rail into the sea.

The cook and his assistants in the galley, preparing food for the next meal.

Boiling up rock-hard chunks of salt meat, and skimming off the fat to make crude candles.

At table in the Great Cabin, the officers eat the same food as the crew members.

Cleaning one of the swivel guns at the rail, to keep it ready for immediate action.

Directed by a gunner's mate, one of the gun crews goes through the firing drill.

(5) Surgeon, with bone saw and medicine chest.
(6, 7) A pair of seamen or 'mariners', caught playing dice instead of working.

(8) The master gunner, in charge of all guns, their carriages and tackle.
(9) A captain of foot soldiers. (10) Ship's boy on a job for the 'swabber', responsible for keeping the ship clean. (11) Cook.

Two crewmen at routine work, scrubbing decks and replacing worn sections of rigging.

Up aloft, two crewmen prepare to set the topsail while the lookout keeps watch.

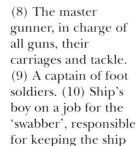

THE NAVIGATOR

O N LONG OCEAN VOYAGES, the skills of the navigator were vital. If he got his sums wrong and plotted a faulty position or course for the ship, the whole crew could die of thirst and hunger far out at sea.

In familiar waters, close to land, navigators used the 'three Ls': landmarks, lead-line and log. The navigator steered from landmark to landmark, checking them off on his chart. Dropping a lead weight on a marked line showed the depth of water beneath the ship. From sea-bed samples, brought up on the tallow-filled base of the lead, an experienced navigator could tell where the ship was. Counting the knots in the log-line as it unreeled showed the ship's speed.

Out at sea, the navigator had to calculate the ship's latitude – its position north or south of the Equator. To do this he measured the sun's height above the horizon at noon, or that of the Pole Star at night, using an astrolabe, a cross-staff or a quadrant. The east–west position or longitude was worked out using the distance sailed from the port of departure. Compass and log gave the direction and speed; time was measured by turning sandglasses.

Right: A traverse-board was used during each 4-hour watch to record changes of course. Working outwards from the centre, a new peg was put in every half-hour to show the course being steered and help calculate the ship's position. Dividers were used for marking equal distances on the chart. Time at sea was measured by turning sandglasses. Each one measured the passing of 30 minutes.

The three Ls

Log-line

Landmarks

Lead-line

Log-line

Using the 'three Ls'; lookouts find shore landmarks, the lead-line measures water depth, and the log measures the ship's speed. Left: A log-line on its reel. Counting the knots that ran out after the log had been dropped into the sea gave the speed. Ship speeds are still measured in 'knots' today. Below: Leads for taking depth-measurements, known as soundings.

Log

Hollow base full of tallow

Leads

This handsome Italian compass (right) has its own ivory case and lid.

Traverse board

Sandglasses

Dividers

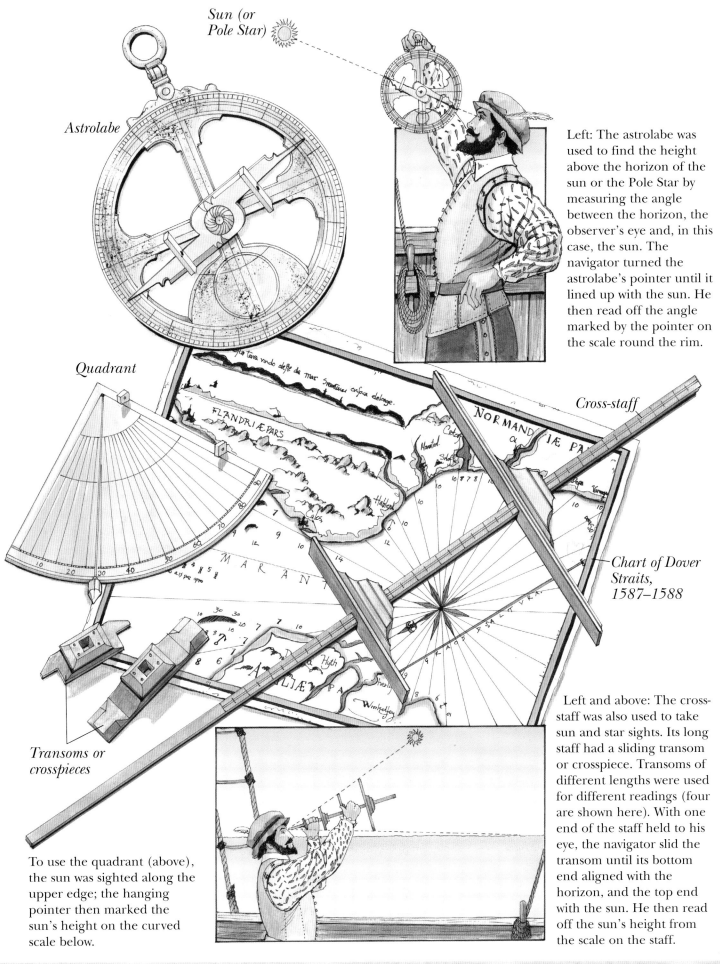

Sun (or Pole Star)

Astrolabe

Quadrant

Transoms or crosspieces

Chart of Dover Straits, 1587–1588

Cross-staff

Left: The astrolabe was used to find the height above the horizon of the sun or the Pole Star by measuring the angle between the horizon, the observer's eye and, in this case, the sun. The navigator turned the astrolabe's pointer until it lined up with the sun. He then read off the angle marked by the pointer on the scale round the rim.

To use the quadrant (above), the sun was sighted along the upper edge; the hanging pointer then marked the sun's height on the curved scale below.

Left and above: The cross-staff was also used to take sun and star sights. Its long staff had a sliding transom or crosspiece. Transoms of different lengths were used for different readings (four are shown here). With one end of the staff held to his eye, the navigator slid the transom until its bottom end aligned with the horizon, and the top end with the sun. He then read off the sun's height from the scale on the staff.

THE GALLEON IN BATTLE

WHEN THE NEW GALLEONS were first used in battle in the 1570s, they displayed several advantages over the two types of warship in use until then. The oar-powered galley only had its light guns and its pointed bow for making ramming attacks; the 'great ship', of 700 tons or more, was towering but slow.

Galleys only had one chance of beating a galleon: to attack in a flat calm, firing at an angle on which the galleon could not fire back. But even a becalmed galleon could launch its boats, to tow the galleon round until its broadside guns were on target.

Galleon captains learned to seize one vital advantage right at the beginning of a fight: the weather gage. This meant getting upwind of the enemy before the first shot was fired. Once he had the weather gage, a galleon's captain could fight the battle as he chose.

Against 'great ships', a galleon with the weather gage could attack the enemy's upwind side. Because this side lacked the shelter enjoyed by the downwind side, the lower gunports would be closed against the sea, preventing any firing. The faster-turning galleon could usually hit with two broadsides before a 'great ship', although armed with more guns, had managed to fire one.

Few galleons were sunk in battle by enemy gunfire. Gunners fired to cripple enemy ships by damaging their rigging and bringing down their masts and spars. Every shot striking home on an enemy hull punched out a flying spray of jagged wooden splinters. These caused terrible injuries, especially if the ship's decks were packed with soldiers.

A galleon might carry as many as 36 guns. There would be 16 culverins on the lower deck, 12 demi-culverins on the upper deck, and 8 even lighter guns, called sakers, in the waist and on the aft half-deck.

A typical 30-gun galleon had a crew of about 180. In battle, 66 of them would fire the guns, 50 would man the small arms on the upper deck, and 50 would sail the ship and 'man the tops' up the masts.

There would be 4 men in the powder room, and up to 4 carpenters below to repair damage and plug shot-holes. The surgeon and his mates would be tending the wounded, and the rest of the crew would be standing by to put out any fires caused in battle.

Good seamanship, using the galleon's sailing qualities to out-manoeuvre the enemy, won many a battle at sea. In the battle shown here, two galleons, their sails pocked with shot holes, are steering upwind to capture the all-important weather gage from the enemy.

TRADE AND PLUNDER

ETWEEN 1488 AND 1522, the great voyages of Diaz, Columbus, da Gama and Magellan had placed the riches of the East and West Indies in the hands of Portugal and Spain. One hundred years later, however, it was a very different story. The sea power won by the fighting galleon had enabled England and Holland to seize their share of those riches. While the Dutch won control of the Far East trade from the Portuguese, the English set up their first colonies in North America.

New vegetables and fruits were shipped from the west Indies and America: potatoes and tomatoes, maize (sweetcorn) and kidney beans, chilli peppers, sweet peppers and pineapples. Less nourishing, but no less profitable, was tobacco as the craze for smoking took hold in Europe.

But the richest single prizes were the great cargo ships carrying American gold and silver and Far Eastern spices back to Spain. In June 1587, the expedition in which Francis Drake 'singed the King of Spain's beard' by attacking Cádiz, ended when he captured the trading carrack *San Felipe*, homeward bound to Spain from the East Indies. When sold in England, her cargo paid twice over for the cost of sending out Drake's fleet.

Roanoke Indians (above) and English settlers of the first Virginia colony on Roanoke island, 1585–1587. Planned by Sir Walter Raleigh and led by Sir Richard Grenville, this was the first English attempt to settle on the North American continent. The pioneer fort and village of Jamestown, Virginia (below), was established in 1607. Though nearly wiped out by hunger and sickness in its early years, the colony survived and eventually flourished.

Some of the New World crops which became known to Europeans in the 16th and 17th centuries. The fiery peppers of Central America provided a new spice trade, and smoking tobacco soon became fashionable. The first tobacco was sold in Europe by apothecaries, or chemists.

(1) Tobacco. (2) Potatoes. (3) Tomatoes. (4) Sweet peppers (capsicums). (5) Hot peppers (chillies). (6) Maize. (7) Kidney beans. (8) Pineapple.

Right: In the 17th century, the East Indies spice trade and a growing trade with China both did well. Chinese porcelain and China tea were brought to Europe.

(1) Cinnamon. (2) Ginger.
(3) Pepper. (4) Coriander.
(5) Cloves. (6) Nutmeg and mace.
(7) Porcelain.
(8) Chinese tea-carrier.

Below: A short-cut to riches – preparing to attack a treasure-ship.

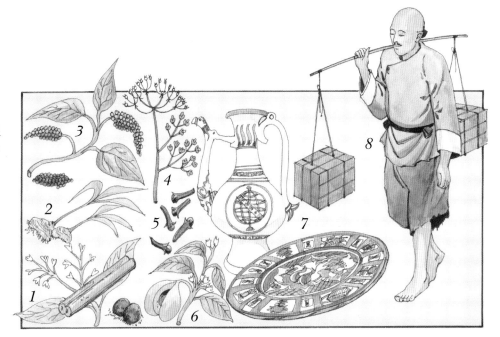

AFTER THE GALLEON

Right: Sweden's *Vasa* (1628) was a 64-gun warship with two gundecks. A landsome ship, decorated with much fine carving, she was built too narrow and too top-heavy. As *Vasa* sailed across Stockholm harbour on her first voyage, she rolled in the first gust of wind. The sea rushed into her lower gunports and she sank like a stone. In 1961, after 333 years on the seabed, *Vasa* was raised to be restored as a museum ship. Like *Mary Rose*, the *Vasa* also contained many well-preserved everyday items that show what life on board must have been like.

THE GALLEON had reached the peak of its development by about 1620, and the biggest ships built after that date were of two types. The first of these was the heavy ship of war, the largest of which had 100 guns or more on three decks. The second was the large merchant ship, armed with at least one deck of guns to defend the costly cargoes that it carried to Europe from East and West. These ships, built for the Eastern trading companies of Europe's sea powers, were called 'East Indiamen'.

Below: Britain's 100-gun *Victory* was launched in 1765, but not completed until 1778. She is now the only surviving three-decked sailing battleship in the world.

Victory served in many sea battles before she became Nelson's famous flagship. Here she is shown in action during the Battle of Trafalgar (21 October 1805) against the fleets of France and Spain. Today *Victory* is preserved in dry dock at Portsmouth on the south coast of England, and is open to the public.

Left: The German *Preussen*, built in 1902 with a steel hull, five steel masts and steel cable shrouds. Carrying 47 sails, she was the biggest-ever square-rigged ship.

The age of sail put up a brave fight against the coming of steam power for ships in the 19th century. The fastest of all the cargo-carrying sailing ships were the clippers. These resisted the challenge of the new steamers from about 1840 to 1869. The fastest clippers could carry tea cargoes from China to Europe in 99 days. But in 1869 the opening of the Suez Canal, which sailing ships could not use, gave steamers an unbeatable short-cut from the East.

Big steel sailing ships with five masts or more, rigged with steel cable instead of hemp ropes, were still being built as the 20th century began. But many were wrecked, or sunk by submarines in the First World War of 1914–1918, after which the victory of steam over sail was complete.

This cutaway view shows how tea chests were crammed into a clipper's narrow hull.

Below: The British clipper *Cutty Sark* made her first voyage in 1870. She survived many storms and is now preserved at Greenwich, London, but was badly damaged by fire in 2007.

TIMESPAN

1571 The last great sea fight between fleets of galleys was the Battle of Lepanto, fought between Turkish and Christian fleets off the Greek coast in October 1571.

1577 One of the first of the new-style fighting galleons built in England was *Revenge* (34 guns, 441 tons).

1582 The first sea battle won by a fleet of galleons was a Spanish victory. It was fought off Terceira in the North Atlantic Azores Islands in July 1582.

1587 On 18 June, in the galleon *Elizabeth Bonaventure*, Sir Francis Drake captured his richest prize. She was the Portuguese merchant ship *San Felipe*, and her cargo of spices, silks, and ivories was worth an immense fortune.

1588 The heaviest ship in the Spanish Armada was the *Reganzona*, of 1,294 tons. The heaviest English ship was the *Triumph*, of 1,100 tons.

1588 In four battles with the English fleet, only one galleon of the Spanish Armada was sunk by gunfire (the *María Juan*, lost off Flanders on 8 August).

1591 In the long sea war with Spain, only one English galleon was lost. This was the *Revenge*, captured off Flores in the Azores in April 1591 after a desperate fight against 15 Spanish galleons.

GLOSSARY

Astrolabe Instrument for finding the altitude of the sun or a star, to fix the ship's latitude.

Ballast Heavy stones packed in a ship's bilge to hold the ship upright in the water.

Bilge The lowest part of a ship inside the hull.

Bonaventure (or **counter-mizzen**) A small fourth mast, right at the stern of the ship.

Bonnet A strip of sailcloth laced to the bottom of the larger sails for more power in steady or 'fair' winds.

Bowsprit Spar extending from the bow to brace the fore-topmast and carry a spritsail.

Broadside The number of guns mounted to fire through gunports cut in a ship's side.

Bunt The central part of a square sail.

Caravel Small 15th-century trading ship, used in early ocean exploration.

Carrack Large trading ship of the 14th–17th centuries, with four masts.

Carvel-building Shipbuilding by laying a smooth skin of planks edge to edge over a framework.

Caulkers Men whose job was to fill the joins or seams between planks with waterproof material.

Clews The bottom corners of a square sail.

Clinker-building Shipbuilding by forming a shell of overlapping planks and inserting a relatively light framework to brace it.

Cog 13th- to 14th-century trading ship, clinker-built with single mast and sail.

Compass Instrument for finding the direction of magnetic North (close to the North Pole) and hence the direction in which a ship is sailing.

Cooper Craftsman responsible for making and repairing the barrels and casks used for storing food, water and gunpowder.

Courses The lowest and largest sails carried by a ship.

Cross-staff A navigation instrument for finding latitude.

Culverin A medium-sized gun firing a shot of about 7.5 kg.

Deadeyes Thick wooden discs around which the lower ends of ropes are spliced.

Demi-cannon Heaviest gun carried by galleons, firing a shot of about 14.5 kg.

Demi-culverin Gun firing a shot of about 4 kg.

Earing A small rope fastening the upper corners of a square sail to the yard.

Fashion-pieces Curved timbers forming the edges of a ship's stern.

Fibres The finest element of rope, spun right-handed to form yarn.

Floor timbers The timbers across the keel which shape the flat underside of a ship.

Fo'c'sl (pronounced 'FOAK-sull') Sailor's pronunciation of 'forecastle'.

Foot The bottom edge of a square sail.

Foremast The front mast of a ship.

Frames The curved ribs of a ship.

Futtocks Pieces of timber joined together to make a ship's frame.

Gooseneck The hinge connecting the whipstaff to the tiller.

Gunports Square holes cut through the outer planking of a ship and fitted with hinged lids, allowing guns to be fired in broadsides.

Hafskip An ocean-going Viking ship.

Head The upper edge of a square sail.

Helm Another name for the tiller.

Helmsman The man who steers the ship by means of the tiller.

Keel The long timber forming the ship's backbone, supporting the stem, frames and sternpost.

Knees Strong timber brackets fixing the deck supports to the frames.

Lateen A triangular sail supported by a slanting yard.

Latitude Ship's position measured in degrees north or south of the Equator.

Lead, sounding Lead weight with soft tallow in its hollow base for taking seabed samples, dropped on a marked line to measure the depth of water beneath the ship.

Leech The side of a square sail.

Linstock Holder for a piece of burning match, used to fire guns.

Log Flat piece of wood on a knotted line, trailed from a ship to calculate speed.

Longitude A ship's position measured in degrees east or west of a known point.

Mainmast A ship's tallest and strongest mast, between foremast and mizzenmast.

Mitre The seam joining the two main sections of a triangular sail.

Mizzenmast The third mast of a ship, aft of the mainmast.

Mould-loft A shed with a large floor on which the frames of a new ship are shaped from the builder's designs.

Orlop deck The lowest deck of a ship, below the waterline.

Parrel Heavy rope girdle with wooden slats and roller-bearings, used to fasten the yard to the mast.

Pintles The hooked pins on which the rudder hangs from the sternpost.

Poopdeck Small upper deck at the top of a ship's stern.

Port The left-hand side of a ship, looking towards the bow.

Quadrant Instrument for finding the height of the sun or a star above the horizon.

Quarterdeck Upper deck of the ship's sterncastle from which the ship was commanded, running aft from the mainmast.

Ratlines Thin ropes running across the shrouds, forming steps for men climbing or working aloft.

Robbands The fastenings that lace a square sail's head to the yard.

Rope-walk A long piece of ground set aside for twisting fibres together to make rope.

Rudder A hinged flat timber or structure, moved by the tiller to change a ship's direction.

Running rigging The ropes and tackle, running through blocks and pulleys, that work a ship's sails.

Serving mallet Mallet with hollow rounded face used to *serve*, or wrap, a rope with an outer layer of yarn.

Spar A long wooden pole.

Spritsail Square sail attached to a yard hung from the bowsprit.

Square-rigged ship A ship rigged with square sails attached to yards.

Standing rigging Fixed ropes used to support a ship's masts and spars.

Starboard The right-hand side of a ship, looking towards the bow.

Stays Strong guy-ropes running between the masts and supporting them.

Steering oar Short oar with flattened blade mounted on the side of the stern, used to steer ships before invention of the rudder.

Stem Curved timber rising from the front end of the keel, forming the central timber of the bows.

Stern-chaser A gun firing aft through the ship's stern.

Sternpost A ship's rearmost timber, rising from the rear end of the keel.

Strands The main elements of rope, spun from yarns and fibres.

Tiller Bar fixed to the top of the rudder to move it from side to side in order to steer the ship.

Topgallant mast Light upper mast fixed above the topmast.

Topmast Mast fixed between the lower mast and the topgallant mast.

Topsails Sails set above the lower sails or courses.

Transom Timber running across the sternpost to form the ship's flat stern; also, the sliding cross-piece of a cross-staff.

Traverse board An indicator board marked with the points of the compass, with holes for pegs, showing changes made to a ship's course every 30 minutes.

Trenail mooter Shipyard worker whose craft was the fastening of planking with wooden pegs called trenails.

Weather deck A ship's upper deck (exposed to the weather).

Weather gage The term used for placing a ship upwind of another ship or fleet to gain an advantage in battle.

Whipstaff A vertical lever, connected to the tiller by the gooseneck, used to steer ships before steering wheels came into use.

Yard Strong spar fixed to masts and bowsprit to support a sail.

Yarn String-like line spun from hemp fibres and twisted into strands to make a rope.

INDEX

Page numbers in bold type refer to illustrations.

Created and produced by The Salariya Book Company and first published in MCMXCIII by Simon & Schuster Young Books.

Look out for these other exciting titles from Book House

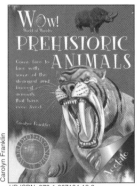

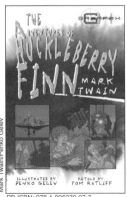

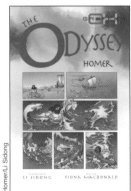
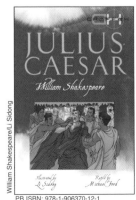